The story of the great feast

Story by Penny Frank
Illustrated by Tony Morris

THE LION
STORY BIBLE

41

OXFORD · BATAVIA · SYDNEY

The Bible tells us how God sent his Son Jesus to show us what God is like and how we can belong to God's kingdom.

This is a story Jesus told to help people understand God's invitation to his kingdom.

You can find the story in your own Bible in Luke's Gospel, chapter 14.

Copyright © 1985 Lion Publishing

Published by
Lion Publishing plc
Sandy Lane West, Littlemore, Oxford, England
ʿSBN 0 85648 766 X
ᴣBN 0 7459 1786 0 (paperback)
Lion Publishing Corporation
1705 Hubbard Avenue, Batavia, Illinois 60510, USA
ISBN 0 85648 766 X
Albatross Books Pty Ltd
PO Box 320, Sutherland, NSW 2232, Australia
ISBN 0 86760 551 0
ISBN 0 7324 0106 2 (paperback)

First edition 1985, reprinted 1986, 1987, 1988
Paperback edition 1989

British Library Cataloguing in Publication Data

Frank, Penny
 The story of the great feast –
 (The Lion Story Bible; 41)
 1. Great supper *(Parable)* – Juvenile
literature
 I. Title
 226'.809505   BT378.G7

 ISBN 0-85648-766-X
 ISBN 0-7459-1786-0 (paperback)

Printed in Yugoslavia

Library of Congress Cataloging in Publication Data

Frank, Penny.
 The story of the great feast.
 (The Lion Story Bible; 41)
 1. Great supper (Parable) – Juvenile
literature. [1. Great supper (Parable)
 2. Parables. 3. Bible stories – N.T.]
 I. Morris, Tony, ill. II. Title.
 III. Series: Frank, Penny. Lion Story
Bible; 41.
 BT378.G7F7 1985   226'.409505
 84-25026
 ISBN 0-85648-766-X
 ISBN 0-7459-1786-0 (paperback)

Jesus often spent time with ordinary people. But sometimes he was invited to the homes of the rich rulers. He told them about God's kingdom too.

One day he was invited to a meal at a rich man's house. While they were all eating, Jesus told them this story.

4

There was once a rich man who was planning to give a great feast. He had made a long list of all the people he was going to invite.

His servants worked hard preparing for the feast. They cooked the food and bought the wine. They decided where each person should sit around the enormous table, and they decorated the room with flowers.

When all the work was finished, the rich
man was pleased with what they had
done.

'Now you can take a message to all
the invited guests,' he told them.

The message said, 'Come to the great feast now. Everything is ready.'

The servants thought that each guest would be waiting in his best clothes, ready to come. But they had a surprise.

One of the servants arrived at the home of the first invited guest.

'The master says, come to the great feast now. Everything is ready,' the servant told him.

'Oh, but I can't come now,' said the first invited guest. 'I've just bought a new field and I must go and see what it is like.'

'That's a poor excuse,' thought the servant. 'Imagine buying a field without looking at it first.' And he went away.

The servant arrived at the house of the second invited guest.

'The master says, come to the great feast now. Everything is ready,' the servant told him.

'Oh, but I can't come now,' said the second invited guest. 'I've just bought five pairs of oxen for my farm work. I must go and try them out.'

'That's a poor excuse,' thought the servant. 'Imagine buying five pairs of oxen for farm work without trying them out first.' And he went away.

The servant arrived at
the home of the third invited guest.

'The master says, come to the great
feast now. Everything is ready,' the
servant told him.

'Oh, but I can't come now,' said the
third invited guest. 'I've just got married,
so I can't go to a feast.'

'That's a poor excuse,' thought the
servant. 'Imagine not going to a feast
just because you have a wife.' And he
went away.

When the servant had been to the homes
of all the guests on the list, he went
back to his master.

The rich man was standing at the
door of his beautiful home. He was
waiting to welcome all his guests.

'Where are they all?' he asked his
servant.

14

The servant explained that when he had told them the great feast was ready they had all made excuses not to come.

The rich man was furious. 'What rude, bad-mannered people,' he shouted.

He went inside and looked at the feast.
The tables were laid and the food
smelled delicious.

'I know what I'll do,' he said.

'Go out into the town,' he said to the servant. 'Look along every street and alley and bring back the poor and the blind and the crippled. Tell them to come to my feast.'

The servant rushed out into the town and did as he was told. Soon the road to the house was full of poor, sick people coming from the town to the feast.

'That's not enough,' said the rich man to his servant. 'There's room for more. Hurry out into the country lanes. Tell everyone you find there to come to my feast.'

So the servant ran out into the country
lanes and did as he was told. The people
there could hardly believe their ears.
They hurried to the feast.

Jesus said, 'In the end the feast was full of people who really wanted to be there.

'Those who couldn't be bothered to come did not have a chance to change their minds.

'That is how it is in God's kingdom,' he said to the people sitting at the table with him. 'When God invites you to belong to him, be sure you say yes.'

The Lion Story Bible is made up of 52 individual stories for young readers, building up an understanding of the Bible as one story — God's story — a story for all time and all people.

The New Testament section (numbers 31–52) covers the life and teaching of God's Son, Jesus. The stories are about the people he met, what he did and what he said. Almost all we know about the life of Jesus is recorded in the four Gospels — Matthew, Mark, Luke and John. The word gospel means 'good news'.
     The last four stories in this section are about the first Christians, who started to tell others the 'good news', as Jesus had commanded them — a story which continues today all over the world.

The story of the great feast comes from the New Testament, Luke's Gospel, chapter 14. It is a parable — a story with a hidden meaning. Jesus came to bring us all an invitation to God's kingdom. We can accept, or we can make excuses. But if we say no, if other things seem more important, we may find the opportunity has gone for ever.
     The next story in the series, number 42: *The story of the lost sheep*, shows how much God cares for every one of us.